DATE DUE

AFRICAN-
AMERICAN
COLLECTIVE
BIOGRAPHIES

Incredible African-American Jazz Musicians

Stephen Feinstein

Enslow Publishers, Inc.
40 Industrial Road
Box 398
Berkeley Heights, NJ 07922
USA

http://www.enslow.com

Library of Congress Cataloging-in-Publication Data

Feinstein, Stephen.
  Incredible African-American jazz musicians / Stephen Feinstein.
    p. cm. — (African-American collective biographies)
  Includes bibliographical references and index.
  Summary: "Readers will learn about a variety of African American jazz musicians including
Louis Armstrong, Duke Ellington, Ella Fitzgerald, Dizzy Gillespie, Charlie Parker, Miles Davis,
John Coltrane, and Herbie Hancock"—Provided by publisher.
  ISBN 978-1-59845-137-5
  1. African American jazz musicians—Biography—Juvenile literature. 2. Jazz musicians—
United States—Biography—Juvenile literature. I. Title.
  ML3929.F45 2011
  781.65092'396073—dc22
  [B]
                                  2010025167
Future editions
Paperback ISBN 978-1-4644-0036-0
ePUB ISBN 978-1-4645-0943-8
PDF ISBN 978-1-4646-0943-5

Printed in the United States of America

032012 Lake Book Manufacturing, Inc., Melrose Park, IL

10 9 8 7 6 5 4 3 2 1

To Our Readers: We have done our best to make sure all Internet addresses in this book were
active and appropriate when we went to press. However, the author and the publisher have
no control over and assume no liability for the material available on those Internet sites or
on other Web sites they may link to. Any comments or suggestions can be sent by e-mail to
comments@enslow.com or to the address on the back cover.

♻ Enslow Publishers, Inc., is committed to printing our books on recycled paper. The paper
in every book contains 10% to 30% post-consumer waste (PCW). The cover board on the outside of each book contains 100% PCW. Our goal is to do our part to help young people and
the environment too!

Photo Credits: Associated Press, pp. 25, 42, 51, 52, 88, 93; Courtesy of Stephanie Fryer,
p. 5; Everett Collection, pp. 8, 11, 61, 67, 73, 91; The Granger Collection, New York, p. 30;
© Hervé Gloaguen/RAPHO/Everett Collection, p. 83; Library of Congress, pp. 14, 21, 37,
47, 57; Mary Evans/Ronald Grant/Everett Collection, p. 19; Photo by Larry Shaw/Rex Fea-
tures/courtesy Everett Collection, p. 32; Redferns/Getty Images, p. 81; Rue des Archives/The
Granger Collection, New York. pp. 41, 63, 71, 78.

Cover Illustration: Everett Collection

Contents

Introduction

Jazz is the first art form invented in America. Created mainly by poor black men and women, it was African Americans' gift to the world. According to writer Gerald Early, jazz is one of America's most important contributions to world culture. Early wrote, "I think there are only three things that America will be known for two thousand years from now: the Constitution, jazz music, and baseball, the three most beautifully designed things this country ever produced."[1]

Jazz did not just appear out of the blue. It is not as if a very clever musician sat down one day and came up with a brand-new type of music. Jazz grew out of a combination of elements from earlier forms of African-American music and European musical traditions. Chief among these were ragtime and the blues. Ragtime had its origins in the 1880s. It was an African-American musical form featuring syncopated rhythms. The name "ragtime" literally means "ragged time." It came from the music's ragged rhythms, or syncopation. In music that has syncopation, players put accents or emphasis on the weak beat, or just before or after the beat.

Compared to European music, according to author James Haskins, ragtime

> was closer to the rhythms of the black dancers who used their heels to make drum sounds, or to that of the black church singers who could vary the rhythms of a Christian hymn so much that a white Christian could not even recognize it. It was also related to the call-and-response pattern of Negro work songs and to the percussive rhythms of the banjo and the bones.[2]

(The bones were actually animal bones that had been cleaned and allowed to dry white in the sun.

4

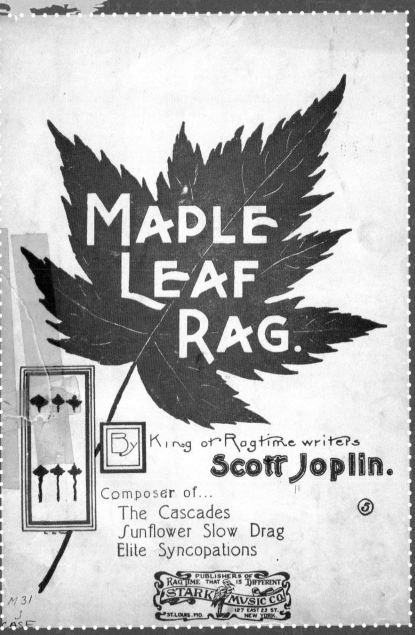

Music for Scott Joplin's hit, "Maple Leaf Rag," one of the most popular rags ever written. Many people consider ragtime to be the first jazz.

When played, the bones made a *clackety-clack* sound to accompany the drum.)

African-American pianist-composer Scott Joplin (1868–1917) became the best-known ragtime composer. His "Maple Leaf Rag," written in 1899, became America's most popular piano rag. Joplin came to be called the Ragtime King. Pianist Eubie Blake (1883–1983), another major ragtime musician, composed, played, and recorded ragtime until late in his life.

Many contemporary music historians consider ragtime to be the first jazz music. But others disagree. Ragtime had the syncopated rhythmic patterns of jazz. But it lacked other elements typical of most jazz music, mainly the blues, swing, and improvised solos.

Since the days of slavery, African Americans in the South had been singing songs of sorrow, loneliness, defiance, and humor. According to James Haskins, the blues were derived from these earlier types of songs:

> *Like the sorrow songs of the earlier plantation slaves, the blues represented the cries of people who had nothing, who seemed to get nothing no matter how hard they tried, and whose lives seemed hopeless. By this time, such songs were often sung in lively rhythms—like laughing to keep from crying.*[3]

The typical format of a blues song was a twelve-bar melody consisting of three different chords. Each bar, or measure, had a fixed number of beats, usually four. Usually, within the twelve bars, a line of music or lyrics was repeated twice, with a closing line contrasting to the first two. Blues is the most basic structure for improvising in jazz. Improvisation is the spontaneous creation of melodies and rhythms. When playing a jazz tune, which may or may not be a familiar song, the player uses the given melody and chord changes as a framework and starting point for exploring the possibilities of the song. As much as half of a jazz performance may be created on the spot.

Introduction

Jazz is said to swing when the strong beat, through the use of syncopation, bombards the listener. Jazz music is characterized by the swing feel. As if to announce this fact to the world, the great jazz composer Duke Ellington wrote a song called "It Don't Mean a Thing (If It Ain't Got That Swing)." Indeed, some believe that the term *swing* originated with that hit tune.

The greatest jazz musicians each had their own voice, sound, or style of playing. Miles Davis played trumpet in a muted whisper. Charlie Parker's saxophone solos displayed phenomenal speed and variety. According to writer Grover Sales, "jazz soloists must improvise at breathtaking tempos that would challenge, and on some instruments excel, the technique, let alone the imagination, of top symphony musicians."[4] That is why jazz improvisation requires a high level of technical and creative ability.

The earliest jazz originated in New Orleans. Its musical elements were derived from African-American brass marching bands and ragtime music from the saloons. Known as Dixieland, it was characterized by several musicians simultaneously playing their improvisations based on the melody and chord pattern of the tune. The tune would most likely have been a popular song of the day or a blues that the musicians did not compose. Many of these early jazz musicians could not read music. But through improvisation they created exciting, joyful music that bore little resemblance to the original tune.

Among the first African-American jazz players were musicians such as Buddy Bolden, Freddie Keppard, Bunk Johnson, and Clarence Williams. Most of these men could not earn a living with their music and were forced to work at menial jobs to get by. A second wave

The Preservation Hall Jazz Band in New Orleans, photographed in the 1960s. This group plays Dixieland, an early type of jazz.

of New Orleans jazz musicians including Joe "King" Oliver, Kid Ory, and Jelly Roll Morton developed the music further and gained greater commercial success than the older players.

Jazz's first important soloists, such as King Oliver and Louis Armstrong, began their careers improvising in these popular Dixieland bands. The music they played was mostly party music, music made for dancing—as jazz would be for many years to come.

Ironically, although African-American musicians laid the groundwork, the all-white Original Dixieland Jass Band (ODJB) made the first jazz record. In 1917, ODJB recorded "Livery Stable Blues."

Introduction

During the 1920s, the center of jazz innovation and excitement migrated from New Orleans to Chicago. That city's bustling clubs and recording studios gave jazz musicians a route to national recognition. Trumpeter Louis Armstrong became jazz's first famous soloist. Because he was such a brilliant improviser, Armstrong brought about a new approach to jazz. Instead of the Dixieland style of group improvisation, now each musician took a solo so that the audience could more fully appreciate and enjoy the creativity and skill of the individual musicians. By the late 1920s, New York had become the heart of the music industry. And by the end of the decade, jazz was a part of America's national culture.

In the 1930s, bandleaders such as Duke Ellington and Count Basie played a style of jazz known as swing. Live radio broadcasts helped make the music popular. Featuring sophisticated big band arrangements, swing was not only good to listen to, it was also great dance music. For the next ten years, swing would be the most popular kind of music in America. Jazz singers who appeared with the bands, such as Ella Fitzgerald and Billie Holliday, also became popular.

Big band swing music maintained its popularity during the 1940s. But later in the decade, with the exception of a few groups such as the Duke Ellington Orchestra, the popularity of swing bands began to decline. Ellington, one of America's greatest composers, over the years had transformed his swing band into a jazz orchestra that performed his lengthy concert pieces, such as *Black*, *Brown and Beige*, in venues such as New York's Carnegie Hall.

Other jazz musicians in the 1940s, such as Charlie "Bird" Parker, Earl "Bud" Powell, Thelonious Monk, and John Birks "Dizzy" Gillespie, were creating a new type of jazz that came to be known as "bebop." The new bebop style featured brilliant improvisation built on complex harmonic structures, played at almost impossibly fast tempos. People who wanted to dance

had to go elsewhere. Bebop was for people who wanted to *listen* to music. Bebop was typically performed by small groups— trios, quartets, or quintets. Unlike swing, bebop never became music for a mass audience, but it retained an audience of devoted jazz fans for decades to come.

During the 1950s, as rock 'n' roll became the most popular style of music for young audiences, there were new developments in jazz. In California, a mellow style known as "cool jazz" emerged. Trumpeter Miles Davis recorded *Birth of the Cool*, which featured the laid-back sound of the new cool jazz. A resident of New York, Davis also played a style of jazz known as "hard bop," an offshoot of bebop that was popular in that city.

In the 1960s, saxophonists John Coltrane and Ornette Coleman were the leading figures of a style known as "free jazz." As the name implies, the music was truly free. Because there were few or no rules, free jazz at times could sound quite chaotic. Players no longer had to stick to the usual elements of jazz improvisation, such as melodic themes and chord patterns. The goal of free jazz musicians was to create the most direct expression of feelings in music.

While some musicians in the 1960s followed the free jazz path, others went off in a completely different direction. Inspired by what was happening in rock, Miles Davis assembled a band featuring musicians playing electric instruments. Davis's band played a jazz-rock fusion style of music that mixed jazz with rock, funk, and soul. Herbie Hancock was one of the pianists who played electric piano in Davis's band.

Since the 1960s, jazz musicians have continued to explore the many varieties of traditional and newer forms of jazz. Today many jazz musicians still play jazz tunes that use the same song structure as the traditional twelve-bar blues. They also play their own versions of old standard songs from Broadway shows and all other kinds of popular tunes. Often this music has a blues feel, even if the tune does not follow the twelve-bar

The Count Basie Orchestra at the Savoy Ballroom, Chicago, sometime in the 1940s in Illinois. "Swing" jazz was popular for dancing.

blues pattern. Some musicians play "straight ahead" jazz in the bebop tradition of Charlie Parker. Some, inspired by the music of John Coltrane, continue to explore the world of free jazz.

Jazz-rock continues to bring the powerful sounds and rhythms of rock to the world of jazz. Jazz musicians have also incorporated elements from various musical traditions around the world. Different kinds of fusion jazz combine jazz with Indian, Middle Eastern, and many other types of music. Latin jazz musicians combine elements of Brazilian, Cuban, or Puerto Rican music with jazz. Acid jazz combines sounds from jazz, soul, funk, and even hip-hop. In addition, in recent years, some players, such as Kenny G, have perfected an "easy listening" style of music known as "smooth jazz."

11

Created by African Americans, jazz is now played in every corner of the world, by musicians of every nationality and ethnicity. According to writer Ted Gioia, "This music of one people, then of a nation, is now a world phenomenon, and its history promises to become many histories, many sounds, and many tales yet to unfold."[5] Jazz retains its freshness and appeal because of its inventiveness, expressiveness, liveliness, and spontaneity.

Chapter 1

Louis Armstrong

Once in a while, what seems to be a bad break can turn out to be a stroke of good luck. That is what happened to Louis Armstrong when he was thirteen years old. It was New Year's Eve, 1913. In Louis's neighborhood of New Orleans, it was customary for people to set off fireworks and shoot pistols at midnight. Louis had found a .38-caliber pistol in a trunk belonging to his mother's latest boyfriend. He grabbed the pistol and went outside, where he met some friends.

According to Armstrong:

> Everybody shot their pistols, shotguns, firecrackers, roman candles ... And we went up Rampart Street singing "My Brazilian Beauty," ... And just then a little old [man] across the street pulls out a pistol ... a kid's pistol [and fires]. The [guys] in my quarter said, "Get him Dipper," and I said, "OK"—"Voom! Voom! Voom!" Aww, it was fun. And then all of a sudden two arms hugged me, and I looked up and there was a big tall detective. Boy, I thought the world was coming to an end ... and I cried, "Oh Mister, ... let me alone, just take the pistol."[1]

Louis Armstrong in 1937

The policeman took the pistol. He also took Louis off to jail. The next morning, the juvenile judge sent Louis to a detention center called the New Orleans Home for Colored Waifs. There he would remain for the next year. But during this time, Louis pleaded to participate in the school's uniformed marching band. As luck would have it, the band's director, Peter Davis, decided to take a chance on Louis. He allowed him to try first the tambourine, then the bugle, and finally the cornet. (The cornet is a type of trumpet; it plays in the same key as a regular trumpet but has a mellower sound.) If Louis had never been arrested and sent to the Home, the world might never have heard of him—and the world of jazz might have missed one of the greatest musicians of all time.

One of his biographers wrote that Daniel Louis Armstrong was born in 1898. Others believed he was born in 1899. But a baptismal certificate discovered in the 1980s gives August 4, 1901, as the date of his birth. However, Louis claimed to be born in New Orleans on the Fourth of July in 1900. His father, Willie Armstrong, left his mother, Mary Ann (better known as Mayann), shortly after Louis was born.

Life was difficult for Mayann, Louis, and his younger sister, Beatrice. Mayann sent her children to live with their grandmother for several years. When Louis was five, Mayann moved her children back with her. They lived in a poor section of New Orleans known as Storyville. They often went hungry. Young Louis often had to search for something to eat in garbage cans.

Louis was pretty much left alone on the streets all day. There he hung out with other boys, playing and sometimes fighting. The most exciting moments for Louis occurred whenever a brass marching band would come down the street. Louis loved music. In those days, there was music everywhere in the African-American community. There was music in theaters, in tent shows, at dances, and at parties. Brass marching bands would accompany funeral processions and march in parades. Louis and his friends would run after the bands, singing and dancing along to the music.

Young Louis dreamed of becoming a musician. When he was seven, he got a job working for Morris Karnofsky, who collected rags and old bottles and delivered coal. Louis would ride on Karnofsky's wagon, blowing a tin horn to announce their arrival in the neighborhood. As time went by, Louis wondered what it would be like to blow a real horn.

One day Louis saw an old cornet in the window of a pawnshop. Karnofsky loaned Louis the money to buy it. According to Louis, one of Karnofsky's sons, also named Morris,

> requested me to play a tune on it. Although I could not play a good tune, Morris applauded me just the same which made me feel very good. As a young boy coming up, the people whom I worked for were very much concerned about my future in music. They could see that I had music in my soul. They really wanted me to be something in life. And music was it. Appreciating my every effort.[2]

At age eleven, Louis quit working for Karnofsky and also dropped out of the Fisk School for Boys. He often drifted into trouble on the streets. Then came his "lucky" break at the New Orleans Home for Colored Waifs. While playing cornet in the school's marching band, Louis became so good that he was appointed leader of the group. The band often appeared in public, marching through the streets, and people became aware of Louis's talent.

Louis Armstrong

Louis left the Home in 1914. For the next few years, he worked at a variety of jobs to help support his mother and sister. He unloaded bananas from boats, sold coal, and delivered milk. Several nights a week, after a long day of hard work, Louis would make the rounds of Storyville's honky-tonks. (Honky-tonks were cheap nightclubs or dance halls.) In these clubs, he would sit in with the local bands whenever the cornetist needed a break. Louis learned a lot from the professional musicians he played with. He spent three summers as a member of the band on an excursion boat making round trips up and down the Mississippi River between New Orleans and St. Paul, Minnesota. Louis became a superb blues improviser. In 1918 he married Daisy Parker, but the marriage did not last long.

One day in 1918, Louis sat in with trombonist Edward "Kid" Ory's Sunshine Orchestra. Kid Ory and Joe "King" Oliver, a cornetist in Ory's band, had been developing their own style of Dixieland jazz. Oliver immediately recognized Louis's ability. He befriended the younger player and taught him all about the new music he was creating. When Oliver left New Orleans for Chicago in 1919, Ory hired Louis to replace Oliver in his band. During the next four years, Louis Armstrong became a great Dixieland cornetist while playing with Kid Ory's band.

In 1922, Oliver sent for Armstrong to join his band in Chicago. Armstrong was eager to pursue the new direction his life was taking. But upon arriving at Chicago's Lincoln Gardens, he hesitated. When he heard the fantastic hot music coming from inside, he wondered if he was good enough to play in that band. But finally he went in, and soon he was playing up a storm with the other musicians.

17

According to Armstrong:

> *When we cracked down on the first note that night at the Lincoln Gardens I knew that things would go well for me. When Papa Joe [Oliver] began to blow that horn of his it felt right like old times. The first number went over so well that we had to take an encore. It was then that Joe and I developed a little system for the duet breaks. We did not have to write them down. I was so wrapped up in him and lived so closely to his music that I could follow his lead in a split second. No one could understand how we did it, but it was easy for us and we kept it up the whole evening.*[3]

Louis Armstrong's boyhood dreams were coming true. Joe Oliver was his idol, and Armstrong was thrilled to be playing up north in Chicago with such a great musician. For the next two years, he played with Joe Oliver's Creole Jazz Band. The band's pianist was a woman named Lil Hardin. She had hoped to have a career as a classical concert pianist, but she found it impossible to earn a living playing classical music. In 1924, Armstrong and Hardlin were married. Also that year, Armstrong went to New York to play with Fletcher Henderson's band. He soon attracted a following of jazz lovers.

Jazz trumpeter Max Kaminsky described how Armstrong influenced the other musicians in Henderson's band:

> *No one knew what swing was till Louis came along. It's more than just the beat, it's conceiving the phrases in the very feeling of the beat, molding and building them so that they're an integral, indivisible part of the tempo. The others had the idea of it, but Louis could do it; he was the heir of all that had gone before and the father of all that was to come.*[4]

The young Louis Armstrong. Armstrong learned a great deal from such mentors as King Oliver and Kid Ory.

Back in Chicago the following year, Armstrong put together his own band, called the Hot Five, and made recordings for Okeh Records. His wife Lil was the band's piano player. By this time, Armstrong had switched from cornet to trumpet. He was becoming more famous all the time for his brilliant trumpet solos. In 1926, Armstrong became even more popular when he introduced audiences to his unique vocal style. That year, he recorded his first hit, a song called "Heebie Jeebies," in which he sang nonsense syllables, a style of jazz improvisation known as scat singing.

In 1929, Armstrong went back to New York to star in a Broadway musical called *Hot Chocolates*. Audiences loved his rendition of the Fats Waller song "Ain't Misbehavin'." He was becoming more popular all the time. His career had reached a turning point. Armstrong no longer focused mainly on blues and Dixieland tunes. From now on he played, sang, and recorded popular songs.

After New York, Armstrong toured the country, appearing in California, New Orleans, and Chicago. He played with big bands as well as his own smaller groups. When he appeared onstage, he danced and sang and clowned as well as played. He was becoming one of the most popular entertainers in the world. From 1932 to 1935, Armstrong toured Europe, appearing before royalty. He was met by a crowd of ten thousand people when he arrived in Denmark. While in London, he received the nickname Satchelmouth, which was later shortened to Satchmo. Apparently, somebody noticed that he had a large mouth and that when he played the trumpet, his cheeks puffed out.

Back in the United States, Armstrong began appearing in films in addition to his live performances. In the films, he would usually play a bandleader or musician.

He appeared with Bing Crosby in *Pennies From Heaven* (1936) and *High Society* (1956). In the 1940s, big bands of one or two dozen members were falling out of favor as the swing era was ending. So in 1947, Armstrong formed a six-piece band of top Dixieland and swing musicians called the All Stars. He would continue with this type of group for the rest of his life.

In 1964, Armstrong's vocal version of "Hello, Dolly" rose to the top of the Billboard Top 100 chart, kicking the Beatles out of first place. Armstrong recorded

Armstrong leading his big band in the 1930s. Known as "Satch," Armstrong was to become one of the most popular entertainers in the world.

"What a Wonderful World" in 1968, which also became a huge hit. By this time, Armstrong's warm, gravelly voice as well as his trumpet playing were familiar to millions of people around the world. The U.S. State Department had long since recognized that Armstrong would make an excellent cultural ambassador to other nations. So they sent him on numerous visits to Asia, Africa, and Europe, including the Soviet Union. His performances over the years for the State Department earned Armstrong the nickname "Ambassador Satch."

Armstrong continued touring and performing until his last days. He died of a heart attack on July 6, 1971, at the age of sixty-nine. Honorary pallbearers at his funeral in New York included New York Governor Nelson Rockefeller, New York City Mayor John Lindsay, Frank Sinatra, Duke Ellington, Dizzy Gillespie, Count Basie, Pearl Bailey, Bing Crosby, and Johnny Carson. Millions mourned the passing of the most popular entertainer in the world. In the words of trumpet player Wynton Marsalis, Louis Armstrong "was chosen to bring the feeling and the message and the identity of jazz to everybody. He brought it to all the musicians. He brought it all over the world. He's the embodiment of jazz music."[5]

Louis Armstrong Timeline

August 4, 1901—Louis Armstrong is born in New Orleans.

1913—Armstrong is arrested for shooting off a pistol. He is sent to detention center, where he learns to play cornet.

1919–1922—Armstrong plays cornet in Kid Ory's Dixieland Jazz Band.

1922–1924—Armstrong plays with Joe "King" Oliver's Creole Jazz Band in Chicago.

1925—Armstrong forms his own band, the Hot Five, with his wife, Lil Hardin, on piano. He switches from cornet to trumpet.

1926—Armstrong records the song "Heebie Jeebies," in which he sings scat improvisation.

1929—Armstrong stars in *Hot Chocolates*, a Broadway musical show in New York.

1932–1935—Armstrong tours in Europe.

1947—Armstrong forms the All Stars, a six-piece band of Dixieland and swing musicians.

1964—Armstrong's recording of "Hello, Dolly" rises to top of Billboard Top 100 chart.

1968—Armstrong records "What a Wonderful World."

July 6, 1971—Louis Armstrong dies.

Duke Ellington

His childhood friends called him "Duke." Perhaps it was because his elegant dress, graceful bearing, and good manners suggested a young nobleman. Perhaps it was because the name Ellington rhymed with the Duke of Wellington. His mother doted on him and from his infancy bought him the finest of outfits. At any rate, the nickname Duke would stick with Edward Kennedy Ellington for the rest of his life.

Edward Kennedy "Duke" Ellington was born on April 29, 1899, in Washington, D.C., to Daisy Kennedy Ellington and James Edward "J. E." Ellington. His family lived in a comfortable home not far from the White House. His father worked as a butler in a doctor's home and occasionally catered at the White House. Daisy Kennedy was very religious and took Duke to two church services each Sunday, one Baptist and one Methodist.

The Ellingtons showered their son with affection and love. Both parents played the piano at home. Not surprisingly, young Duke developed a love of music at a very early age. He also liked to draw, and

24

An undated photograph of Duke Ellington

seemed to be quite talented. His parents encouraged him in both areas. At age seven, Duke began taking piano lessons from a woman with the musical name of Marietta Clinkscales.

Throughout his school years, Duke had three main interests—baseball, music, and art. By the time he started high school, art had become the focus of his future career plans. In 1913 Duke entered Armstrong Manual Training High School, a vocational school. There he studied mechanical drawing and design and other aspects of commercial and fine art. But during this time, Duke never dropped his interest in music.

In the summer of 1914, Duke got a job in Asbury Park, New Jersey, as a dishwasher. His boss told him that a great pianist named Harvey Brooks was appearing in Philadelphia. So on the way home to Washington, Duke stopped off in Philadelphia to hear Brooks. He was glad he did, because Brooks made a huge impression on him. According to Duke, "He was swinging, and he had a tremendous left hand, and when I got home I had a real yearning to play."[1]

Back in Washington, while working at a soda fountain, Duke wrote his first composition, a piece called "Soda Fountain Rag." Now he practiced piano every spare moment, determined to learn how to play ragtime and blues. He listened to as many Washington piano players as he could. He would spend time at Frank Holliday's pool hall, where he heard local rag pianists playing the latest tunes. Duke also sneaked into burlesque shows, where pianists played in various popular styles. Ragtime pianists became Duke's heroes, and he dreamed of following in their footsteps.

According to writer Ted Gioia, "Despite his limitations as a pianist—by his own admission, he only knew three or four songs at the time—opportunities to perform, first among friends but soon for pay, were starting to come his way."[2] The more Duke played at parties and dances, the stronger his desire for a career in music grew.

In 1917, the United States entered World War I. Soon Washington was buzzing with people involved in the war effort. Music gigs, or jobs, became plentiful, and musicians were in demand. Duke became very active in music. That year he did gigs with local bands. The following year, on July 2, Ellington married his girlfriend, Edna Thompson. On March 11, 1919, a son, Mercer Kennedy Ellington, was born.

By this time Ellington had formed his own group, the Duke's Serenaders. And he was putting other bands together and renting rooms to hold dances. Soon school became less important to Ellington. He dropped out before earning his diploma. He even turned down a scholarship to study art at the Pratt Institute of Applied Arts in Brooklyn. This was an incredibly important decision. Had he gone on to Pratt to pursue a career in commercial art, the world might never have gotten to enjoy the musical genius of Duke Ellington.

Although music had now become the main focus of his life, somehow Ellington still found time to earn money from art. He started a sign-painting business for which he designed and painted dance posters and various advertising items.

In 1923, Ellington moved to New York City. With him were his friends trumpeter Artie Whetsel, saxophonist Otto "Toby" Hardwick, drummer Sonny Greer, and banjoist Elmer Snowden. Under the leadership of Snowden, they played at the Exclusive Club in Harlem and then

27

at the Hollywood Club in midtown. In February 1924, Snowden left the group to head another band. Ellington became the group's leader, and the band was now called the Washingtonians.

As new musicians were added to Ellington's band, the Ellington sound began to develop. Trumpeter Bubber Miley and trombonist Charlie Irvis used mutes on their horns in such a way as to imitate the sound of the human voice. (A mute is a device attached to a musical instrument to soften or muffle its tone.) White audiences, hearing what to them sounded like primitive growling, referred to the music as "jungle music." According to jazz historian and trumpeter John Chilton:

> The growl effect comes from fitting a small straight
> mute—a cornet mute for trumpet and a trumpet mute
> for trombone—covering the instrument's bell with a
> rubber plunger, the kind used by plumbers, and moving
> it in and out to affect the tone.[3]

In the fall of 1926, Ellington contracted with a brilliant promoter and music publisher, Irving Mills, to be his manager. Mills suggested that the band focus on their new "growl effect" or "jungle style." He also persuaded Ellington to expand his orchestra. So Ellington added trombonist Joe Nanton, trumpeter Louis Metcalf, and saxophonist and clarinetist Harry Carney. Ellington had begun recording his group in 1924. With his new larger band in 1926, Ellington recorded his tune "East St. Louis Toodle-oo." The song became the band's signature tune for the next fifteen years.

In the spring of 1927, the Duke Ellington Orchestra moved into the whites-only Cotton Club in Harlem. There the band accompanied a slick new revue, with "jungle music." (A revue is a variety show with songs, dances, and comedy acts.) Ellington and his musicians would play at the Cotton Club for the next four years. During this period, live CBS radio broadcasts from the club brought Ellington's music to audiences all over the country. Also during these years, Ellington recorded many of his famous hits, including "Black and Tan Fantasy," "The Mooche," "Black Beauty," "Mood Indigo," and "Creole Rhapsody." "Creole Love Call" was Ellington's first composition to use the human voice as an instrument. The singer sang the melody without using lyrics, or words.

In 1931 Ellington and his orchestra left the Cotton Club and began touring the United States and then in Europe, where they played in London and Paris in 1933. Meanwhile, in 1932 Ellington recorded "It Don't Mean a Thing (If It Ain't Got That Swing)" with singer Ivie Anderson, who had joined the band the previous year.

Throughout the 1930s, while Americans struggled to survive the Great Depression, the Duke Ellington Orchestra had plenty of work. Their big band sound, thanks to Ellington's superb arrangements, was very popular. Ellington had a unique way of composing and arranging for his group. He listened carefully to each of his musicians and created music that was especially suited to their strengths. According to Ellington's clarinetist Barney Bigard, "Duke studied his men. He studied their style, how they maneuver with their music, with their playing and everything. And he keeps that in his mind so if he wrote anything for you, it fit you like a glove."[4]

Ellington and his band began appearing in Hollywood movies. Ellington's recordings from this period include "Sophisticated Lady," "Solitude," and "In a Sentimental Mood." Toward the end of the 1930s, Ellington began to tire of swing dance music. He had begun writing extended concert pieces for his orchestra, works that would ultimately be performed in concert halls.

Duke Ellington and his band in 1937. Though the country was in the midst of the Great Depression, the Duke Ellington Orchestra had plenty of work.

30

In 1938, Ellington met the pianist and composer Billy Strayhorn, who joined the Ellington Orchestra the following year. In 1941, Strayhorn's piece "Take the 'A' Train" became the band's new signature tune. The A train route took people to Harlem's Sugar Hill, a neighborhood full of successful African Americans. The song symbolized taking the high road in life.

Also that year, Ellington's son, Mercer, a successful musician in his own right, contributed "Things Ain't What They Used to Be" and other tunes to expand the band's repertoire.

In January 1943, at a concert in New York's Carnegie Hall, Ellington premiered his concert piece *Black, Brown and Beige*. The work in three sections, which ran for almost an hour, is a musical portrait of African-American history. It met with a mixed reaction from audiences and critics, who were not used to the innovative mixing of jazz and classical forms. In the following years, Ellington continued to compose and perform concert pieces at Carnegie Hall and elsewhere.

By the late 1940s, big band swing music was no longer popular. But Ellington managed to keep finding work for his orchestra. He kept making recordings of his music, including his hit "Satin Doll" in 1953. In 1956, the Duke Ellington Orchestra made a dramatic comeback with their performance at the Newport Jazz Festival. Audiences were astounded by tenor saxophonist Paul Gonsalves's marathon twenty-seven-chorus solo on the tune "Diminuendo and Crescendo in Blue," probably the longest solo ever heard up to that time.

Working some three hundred nights every year, Ellington earned five hundred thousand to seven hundred thousand dollars a year. He continued to write, arrange, record, and perform his music for the rest of his life. In 1965, Ellington gave what was billed as his "First Sacred Concert" at Grace Cathedral in San Francisco. The concert was a success, although some people were not pleased to see jazz performed in a church. Later that same year Ellington gave the second Sacred Concert at the Fifth Avenue Presbyterian Church in New York City. And three years later he gave a third Sacred Concert at the New York's Cathedral of St. John the Divine.

In the 1960s and 1970s Ellington and his orchestra toured the world. They visited Japan, Europe, Africa, India, the Philippines, Thailand, Singapore, Indonesia, Australia, the Middle East, and the Soviet Union. Many of his concert tours were sponsored by the U.S. State

Ellington on the set of the movie *Paris Blues* in 1960

Department, which sent him abroad as an ambassador of jazz. In 1969, on Ellington's seventieth birthday, President Richard Nixon gave him the Presidential Medal of Freedom at a dinner in the White House. Ellington received nineteen honorary PhDs.

After collapsing while on tour in Canada, Duke Ellington died in New York on May 24, 1974. More than sixty-five thousand people passed by his casket, and more than ten thousand crowded into the Cathedral of St. John the Divine for his funeral.

Over a fifty-year period, Ellington had given more than twenty thousand performances throughout the world, made hundreds of recordings, and written over two thousand compositions. According to Wynton Marsalis:

> The most important things to know about Duke Ellington are that he loved people, he loved life, and he loved music. He understood that anything is possible. He understood what it took to make something invisible visible, knew how to take what could be and make it what is.[5]

Duke Ellington Timeline

April 29, 1899—Edward Kennedy "Duke" Ellington is born in Washington, D.C.

1913—Ellington enters Armstrong Manual Training High School, where he studies commercial and fine art.

1914—Ellington hears pianist Harvey Brooks play in Philadelphia.

1918—Ellington marries Edna Thompson.

1919—Ellington's son, Mercer Kennedy Ellington, is born.

1923—Ellington plays at Exclusive Club in Harlem in New York, also at Hollywood Club.

1924—Ellington becomes leader of group, now called the Washingtonians.

1926—Ellington records his tune "East St. Louis Toodle-oo."

1927—Ellington Orchestra moves into the Cotton Club in Harlem.

1931–1933—Ellington Orchestra tours United States and Europe.

1932—Ellington records "It Don't Mean a Thing (If It Ain't Got That Swing)."

Timeline

1938—Ellington meets Billy Strayhorn, who joins Ellington's orchestra the following year.

January 1943—Ellington premieres his concert piece *Black, Brown and Beige* at Carnegie Hall in New York City.

1953—Ellington records "Satin Doll."

1956—Ellington Orchestra makes dramatic comeback at Newport Jazz Festival.

1965—Ellington gives his first Sacred Concert at San Francisco's Grace Cathedral.

1960s–1970s—Ellington Orchestra tours the world.

1969—President Richard Nixon gives Ellington the Presidential Medal of Freedom at a dinner in the White House.

May 24, 1974—Duke Ellington dies in New York.

1986—U.S. Postal Service issues a stamp honoring Ellington.

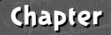

Ella Fitzgerald

"It was a dare from some girlfriends," Ella Fitzgerald recalled. "They bet me I wouldn't go on. I got up there and got cold feet. I was going to dance. The man said since I was up there I had better do something. So I tried to sing like Connee Boswell—'The Object of My Affection.'"[1] It was November 21, 1934, Wednesday Amateur Night at the Apollo Theater in Harlem.

Ella had entered the contest intending to dance. But then she saw that she would have to go on after the Edwards Sisters, a hot dance duo. Ella was intimidated by the Edwards Sisters. Outfitted like professional dancers with sequins on their dresses, they would be a tough act to follow.

At the time, seventeen-year-old Ella was living on the streets after running away from a girl's training school. She wore dirty, ill-fitting clothes and men's shoes, and she had an unkempt appearance. On the Apollo stage, she felt unsure of herself. The Apollo audiences were widely known for their brutally accurate evaluation of talent.

Ella Fitzgerald
in 1964

As Ella began to sing, her voice cracked and she stumbled over the lyrics. The audience began booing. Ella had to start over again. But once she got into the song, her confidence returned. By the time she finished, to her surprise and delight, she brought the house down. When she was called onstage at the end of the evening, the roar of the crowd made it clear that Ella had won the contest. Little did they know that they had just heard the voice of a woman who would become one of the greatest jazz singers of all time—the First Lady of Song.

Ella Fitzgerald was born on April 25, 1917, in Newport News, Virginia, to Temperance (Tempie) and William Fitzgerald. When Ella was three, William left. Tempie, who worked as a laundress, soon had another man in her life, Joseph Da Dilva. In search of a better life, Tempie, Joe, and Ella moved north, where they settled in Yonkers, New York, just north of New York City. In 1923, a daughter, Frances, was born to Tempie and Joe.

Ella's childhood friends remember her as being a happy girl who loved to sing and dance. There did not seem to have been much musical influence at home or at school. According to Ella, "My mother had a very beautiful, classical voice.... But I don't think she ever really did too much of it. They tell me that my father was a guitar player, but I don't know."[2] However, Ella did get to sing at services and Sunday school at the Bethany African Methodist Episcopal Church in Yonkers.

38

Ella's friend Annette Miller remembered Ella as being shy but very ambitious. According to Miller, "She would tell us, 'Someday you're going to see me in the headlines. I'm going to be famous.' We'd all laugh, 'Oh yeah, sure!'"[3]

Ella loved to dance. She would learn the latest dance steps with her friend Charles Gulliver, Annette Miller's brother. When she was fifteen, Ella and Charles began getting dance jobs at clubs around Yonkers. They would earn a few pennies by demonstrating dance steps. Ella thought that someday she would become a famous dancer. According to Charles, "She always knew she was going to be someone someday because she kept on saying, 'I want to do something. I want to make something of myself.' And she did."[4]

Ella had the ability to accurately mimic songs she heard on the radio and on records. She was particularly attracted to the jazz singing styles of Louis Armstrong and Connee Boswell. According to Ella, "When I was a girl, I listened to records by all the singers, white and black, and I know that Connee Boswell was doing things that no one else was doing at the time. You don't have to take my word for it. Just check the recordings and hear for yourself."[5]

In 1932, Tempie died of a sudden heart attack. Ella did not get along well with Joe, so she went to live with her aunt Virginia in Harlem. She dropped out of school. She got into trouble with the police, who took her into custody and sent her to the New York State Training School for Girls, a reform school upstate near Albany. In 1934, Ella ran away from the reform school and was homeless for a while.

It was around this time that she entered the contest at the Apollo Theater. Ella won first prize, which consisted of a week's work performing at the Apollo. Although she won the prize, she was never given the work because of her poor appearance. Not discouraged, Ella kept entering other contests. Eventually, she began making a name for herself. Musicians, as well as music lovers in the audiences, were becoming aware of Ella's talent.

In 1935, drummer and bandleader Chick Webb hired Ella to sing and travel with his swing band. During the next few years, Ella recorded many songs with the Chick Webb Band. Her recording of "A-Tisket, A-Tasket" in 1938 was her first big swing hit. In 1939, Webb died, and Ella became the bandleader. The group's name was changed to Ella Fitzgerald and Her Famous Orchestra.

Fitzgerald left the band in 1942 to begin a solo career. Swing music was going into decline during the 1940s, and Fitzgerald moved to the new bebop style of jazz. She sang with Dizzy Gillespie, among others. She now perfected her scat singing, where she improvised as if her voice were an instrument. Fitzgerald had a vocal range that spanned three octaves. Because an octave consists of eight notes of a scale, she was easily able to sing low notes all the way up to very high notes. Her abilities as an improviser, especially considering the fast tempos and complex chord changes of bebop, were phenomenal. According to composer, arranger, and producer Quincy Jones, "When you listen to Ella, you hear a jazz musician interpreting the melody, blending variations of phrasing, melody, rhythm and spontaneous improvisation. She could use her exquisite, very human voice just like a saxophone, sometimes like a violin, sometimes like a trumpet."[6]

From 1956 to 1964, Fitzgerald was busy recording albums of songs by America's greatest songwriters. The songs of these composers form a body of work known as the Great American Songbook. By moving in this direction, Fitzgerald expanded her already huge base of fans to include a nonjazz audience. Fitzgerald recorded eight multialbum songbook sets that included the songs of Cole Porter, Duke Ellington, Irving Berlin, Richard Rodgers and Lorenz Hart, Harold Arlen, Jerome Kern, George and Ira Gershwin, and Johnny Mercer.

Ella Fitzgerald in concert, 1937. Fitzgerald used her voice like a musical instrument.

During these years, Fitzgerald made additional recordings and also often toured throughout the United
States and Europe, performing for millions of fans. In
1956 and 1957, she recorded three albums with her early
idol Louis Armstrong. The two had great fun working
together.

Ella Fitzgerald in 1992. Her last public performance was a year later.

Ella Fitzgerald

In one famous recording from 1960, *Mack the Knife: Ella in Berlin*, she forgot the lyrics to the title song during a live performance. She compensated for this by dazzling the audience with brilliant improvising.

During her long, successful career, the main thing in Fitzgerald's life was her music. She loved to sing more than anything else, and her greatest happiness came from performing for her fans and making them happy. Her personal life was not as successful. She was married twice, the second time to bass player Ray Brown, from 1947 to 1953.

Fitzgerald's recordings spanned a period of fifty-seven years. On June 18, 1987, President Ronald Reagan awarded Fitzgerald the National Medal of Arts in a ceremony at the White House. Then on December 11, 1992, President George H. W. Bush honored her with the Presidential Medal of Freedom.

In the early 1990s her health began to fail. Fitzgerald made her last recording in 1991 and her last public performance in 1993. Later that year, already blinded by the effects of diabetes, she had both legs amputated. On June 15, 1996, Ella Fitzgerald died of diabetes in Beverly Hills, California, at the age of seventy-nine.

In summing up the essence of Fitzgerald's art, Frank Sinatra said:

> *If Ella were a musical instrument, she'd be the whole damn orchestra. Her pure and almost childlike voice is a melody unto itself. Never have such innocent sounds been set to music nor has such music sounded so effortless. Ella is musical perfection.*[7]

Ella Fitzgerald Timeline

April 25, 1917—Ella Fitzgerald is born in Newport News, Virginia.

1934—Fitzgerald wins amateur night competition at Harlem's Apollo Theater.

1935—Fitzgerald joins Chick Webb's band.

1938—Fitzgerald records her first big swing hit, "A-Tisket, A-Tasket."

1939—Fitzgerald takes over the band when Webb dies. Group is called Ella Fitzgerald and Her Famous Orchestra.

1942—Fitzgerald leaves band to begin a solo career. She moves to bebop jazz, because swing is in decline. She becomes known for amazing scat improvisations.

1947—Fitzgerald marries bass player Ray Brown.

1956–1964—Fitzgerald records eight multialbum songbook sets that include songs by America's greatest songwriters. During these years she tours the United States and Europe.

1956–1957—Fitzgerald records three albums with Louis Armstrong.

1979—Fitzgerald is inducted into the Big Band Jazz Hall of Fame.

Timeline

1987—President Ronald Reagan awards Fitzgerald the National Medal of Arts in ceremony at White House.

1992—President George H. W. Bush awards Fitzgerald the Presidential Medal of Freedom.

1993—Fitzgerald makes last public performance.

June 15, 1996—Ella Fitzgerald dies in Beverly Hills, California.

2007—U.S. Postal Service issues a stamp honoring Fitzgerald.

Dizzy Gillespie

Four-year-old John Birks Gillespie's favorite toys were somewhat unusual. They consisted of an assortment of musical instruments. Among the many instruments in the parlor of the Gillespie home were a piano, clarinet, guitar, mandolin, bass fiddle, and a set of drums. John's father, James, a bricklayer, was also an amateur musician. He was the leader of a local band, and he stored the band's instruments in his home. Of course, these musical instruments were not really John's "toys." But nothing made young John happier than getting his little hands on the various instruments and making sounds on them. Not surprisingly, John would later make history with his exciting jazz sounds.

John Birks Gillespie was born on October 21, 1917, in Cheraw, South Carolina, to James and Lottie Gillespie. He was the youngest of their nine children. While growing up, John had plenty of opportunity to learn about many different kinds of musical instruments. He also got to hear a lot of music, listening to his father's band during rehearsals and performances. Unfortunately, James

46

Dizzy Gillespie in 1955

Gillespie died when John was ten years old. By this time John loved music more than anything else, but there was nobody to guide him.

When he was fourteen, John joined the band at the Robert Smalls High School. He was assigned to play trombone. Although he quickly taught himself the basics of how to produce a sound and play different notes, he switched to the trumpet several months later. His idol at the time was the trumpet player Roy Eldridge. Each week, John listened to radio broadcasts of Teddy Hill's band from New York's Savoy Ballroom. Eldridge was the band's featured trumpet player. John was inspired by Eldridge's exciting solos.

John practiced his horn at every spare moment and taught himself as much as he could about the trumpet. His hard work paid off. In 1933 John won a scholarship to study music at Laurinburg Institute, an African-American vocational school in North Carolina. He continued to develop his trumpet skills at Laurinburg, where he also studied piano and music theory. In 1935, John left Laurinburg shortly before his graduation in order to move to Philadelphia with his family.

In Philadelphia, John had enough confidence in his playing to get gigs with various small groups. Then he joined Frank Fairfax's big band. Trumpet player Charlie Shavers taught him how to play Roy Eldridge's trumpet solos. But he also advised John to develop his own style instead of copying others. While John was playing with the Frank Fairfax Band, the other band members could not help but notice that he was always clowning around. Someone gave him the nickname "Dizzy," and it stuck.

In 1937, Gillespie moved to New York City and joined Teddy Hill's band. He traveled to Europe with the group that summer. He soon became the group's first

trumpet—the featured trumpet soloist. He thus filled the same role that Eldridge had held before him.

The following year, he married Lorraine Willis. In 1939, Gillespie joined Cab Calloway's band. Among the many fine musicians in the group was bass player Milt Hinton. He encouraged Gillespie to keep working on his own original ideas. Gillespie began participating in jam sessions, informal gatherings of musicians to play improvised jazz at Minton's Playhouse, a club in Harlem. There he and other musicians such as pianist Thelonious Monk were developing a new style of jazz that came to be called "bebop."

One day in 1940, when the Cab Calloway band was playing in Kansas City, Gillespie was introduced to a young sax player named Charlie Parker. An impromptu jam session was arranged. According to Gillespie, "I was astounded by what the guy could do.... Charlie Parker and I were moving in practically the same direction too, but neither of us knew it."[1] At the time, Gillespie was playing like Eldridge. But from then on, he began to play more and more like Parker, without intending to copy his style. According to Gillespie, "Lorraine told me one time, 'Why don't you play like Charlie Parker?' I said, 'Well that's Charlie Parker's style. And I'm not a copyist of someone else's music.' But he was the most fantastic musician."[2]

Meanwhile, Gillespie began to have problems with Calloway. According to Gillespie, "Monk and I would work on an idea. Then I'd try it out the next night with Calloway. Cab didn't like it. It was too strange for him."[3] Nor did Calloway appreciate Gillespie's clowning around. Eventually in 1941, the two had a fight, and Calloway fired Gillespie.

Gillespie played briefly with singer Ella Fitzgerald. Then he joined the Benny Carter Sextet. In 1943 Gillespie played with pianist Earl "Fatha" Hines, and the following year with singer Billy Eckstine's band. Charlie Parker was in both of those bands.

During these years, Gillespie and Parker participated in countless jam sessions, informal practice sessions, and rehearsals. Here they established the guidelines for the bebop style of jazz. According to pianist Billy Taylor:

> *Dizzy Gillespie was the organizer. It was he who arranged and taught many bebop melodies to other musicians. He wrote out lines, riffs, interludes, and sometimes complete arrangements and often dictated what each instrument would play, even the rhythm section. Nevertheless, after everyone learned a part, he or she was given the freedom to add individual touches.* [4]

In 1945 Parker and Gillespie left Eckstine's band. They made recordings together and then went to California, where they played for a while at Billy Berg's, a Hollywood club. Unfortunately, the engagement was a flop. Gillespie went back to New York, where he organized a big band to play bebop.

Gillespie recorded many hits, including his compositions "Night in Tunisia" and "Salt Peanuts." He was also involved with a style of music known as Afro-Cuban. He had always loved Latin music and had sought to combine elements of Latin and African rhythms with jazz. According to Gillespie, "the people of the calypso, the rhumba, the samba and the rhythms of Haiti all have something in common from the mother of their music. Rhythm. The basic rhythm, because Mama Rhythm is Africa."[5] His biggest recorded hits along these lines are his compositions "Manteca" and "Tin Tin Deo."

50

Dizzy Gillespie writes an example of bebop music on a blackboard in 1947.

In 1953, someone fell on Gillespie's trumpet, bending the bell upward. Gillespie claimed he could now hear the sound quicker. After that, he had all of his horns made with the bell pointing up, and this became a trademark. From the 1950s on, Gillespie toured constantly. In 1956, the U.S. State Department sent Gillespie and his band on a tour of the Middle East, Asia, Africa, and Eastern Europe. Gillespie brought live jazz to millions of people who

51

Dizzy Gillespie performing in 1989. He said the angle of his trumpet improved the sound.

had never heard jazz before. Like Louis Armstrong and Duke Ellington, Gillespie became an ambassador of jazz.

Always concerned about civil rights issues in the United States, Gillespie threatened to run for president in the 1980s. He said that if elected, he would rename the White House the Blues House and appoint Miles Davis as head of the CIA.[6]

In 1989, Gillespie visited twenty-seven countries, appeared in a hundred U.S. cities, performed with twenty-eight symphony orchestras, and gave three hundred performances. In 1992, he celebrated his seventy-fifth birthday by playing an eight-week gig at a club in New York. He died of cancer on January 6, 1993. Gillespie's message about what he tried to communicate through jazz is just as relevant today as when he spoke these words: "I'm playing the same notes, but it comes out different. You can't teach the soul. You got to bring out your *soul* on those valves."[7]

Dizzy Gillespie Timeline

October 21, 1917—John Birks "Dizzy" Gillespie is born in Cheraw, South Carolina.

1933—Gillespie wins a scholarship to study music at Laurinburg Institute in North Carolina.

1935—Gillespie leaves Laurinburg to move to Philadelphia with his family. He gets various music gigs in Philadelphia.

1937—Gillespie moves to New York and joins Teddy Hill's band.

1938—Gillespie marries Lorraine Willis.

1939—Gillespie joins Cab Calloway's band.

1943—Gillespie plays in Earl "Fatha" Hines's band with Charlie Parker.

1944—Gillespie plays in Billy Eckstine's band with Parker.

1945—Gillespie and Parker leave Eckstine. They go to California, where they play at a Hollywood club. Club gig is a flop. Dizzy goes back to New York.

1953—Someone falls on Gillespie's trumpet, bending bell upward. Horn with bell pointing up becomes Gillespie's trademark.

1956—U.S. State Department sends Gillespie on tour of Middle East, Asia, Africa, and Eastern Europe.

1992—Gillespie celebrates his seventy-fifth birthday by playing an eight-week gig at a club in New York.

January 6, 1993—Dizzy Gillespie dies.

Chapter 5

Charlie Parker

You do not become an accomplished jazz musician overnight. Years of hard work—long hours of practicing every day—are required to gain the theoretical knowledge and technique you need in order to make your mark in the world of jazz. Young Charlie Parker learned this lesson the hard way. Eager to jam with some older jazz musicians, he went to a local club in Kansas City, the High Hat, only to suffer a humiliating setback. According to Parker:

> I had learned to play two tunes in a certain key … the first eight bars of "Lazy River" and I knew the complete tune of "'Honeysuckle Rose."… So I took my horn out to this joint where … a bunch of fellows who I had seen around worked and the first thing they started playing was "Body and Soul."… So I go to playing my "Honeysuckle Rose."… They laughed me off the bandstand. Everybody fell out laughing. I went home and cried and didn't play again for three months.[1]

Fortunately, young Charlie didn't give up. He was determined to prove to himself and others that he had what it took to become a great jazz musician. Practicing the

Charlie Parker, photographed between 1940 and 1955

saxophone became the only thing that mattered. According to Parker, "I put quite a bit of study into the horn.... In fact, the neighbors threatened to ask my mother to move once ... they said I was driving 'em crazy with the horn. I used to put in at least eleven, eleven to fifteen hours a day."[2]

Whenever he learned a new tune, Charlie would learn how to play it in all twelve keys. This way he would always be able to transpose from one key to another in an instant. He studied the recordings of all the great jazz musicians of the day, especially the sax players such as Lester Young. In this way Charlie taught himself how to play jazz.

Charles Christopher Parker, Jr., was born in Kansas City, Kansas, on August 29, 1920, and raised across the river in Kansas City, Missouri. At the time, Kansas City was a wide-open town of dives, honky-tonks, and jazz spots. Charlie was the only child of Charles Parker, Sr., and Adelaide, known as Addie. Charlie's father worked as a tap dancer in vaudeville theater and as a chef on the railroad. He was away from home much of the time Charlie was growing up, and he moved away for good when his son was eleven.

Addie rented out rooms in their home and also worked as a maid. She was devoted to her son and pampered the young boy. When Charlie was eleven, he told his mother he wanted to be a musician. He had heard Rudy Vallee play saxophone on the radio and said he wanted to play like him. So Addie bought Charlie an alto saxophone. He began playing it, but at the time was really not motivated to practice. However, Charlie played alto and baritone sax in his school band.

By the time Charlie was fourteen, he was spending a lot of time hanging out around the doorways of local bars and nightclubs. According to writer Studs Terkel:

> *It was easy for him to sneak into nightclubs and bars through the musicians' entrance, carrying his sax. Often while waiting in the alley, he'd gnaw away at the roast chicken legs he bought from a nearby vendor. An older musician dubbed him "Yardbird." The nickname stuck. Most often he was simply referred to as "Bird."*[3]

It was around this time that Charlie got laughed off the bandstand while trying to jam with the other musicians. After this, he practiced incessantly, learning one tune at a time. Around this time, Charlie was in an auto accident. He was given morphine to ease his pain. He would spend much of the rest of his life obsessed with getting high, especially on heroin.

Addie hoped to save enough money to send Charlie to college. Charlie, however, was not a good student and dropped out of school at the age of fifteen. On July 25, 1936, when he was almost sixteen, Charlie married Rebecca Ruffin. He began playing with the Deans of Swing, a local dance band.

A son, Francis Leon, was born to Charlie and Rebecca on January 10, 1938. By this time, Charlie was unhappy in his marriage. He also was growing bored with the music he played with the Deans of Swing and some other local groups. He felt he was not growing as a musician. For Charlie it was time to expand his horizons. In 1939, Charlie and Rebecca were divorced. Charlie headed for Chicago and from there he moved on to New York City.

Parker's first job in New York was working as a dishwasher for nine dollars a week. At this time he heard Art Tatum, the speed-playing piano virtuoso. Tatum's style greatly influenced Parker. In order to work

as a musician in New York, Parker had to become a member of the musicians' union. Once he got his union card, he was able to work in New York clubs. He got a job with pianist Jay McShann's band, a group he had briefly played with back in Kansas City. The band played in New York and also did gigs in other cities around the country. He stayed with McShann until 1942.

During this time he developed a method of playing the sax that he had been searching for. Parker's big breakthrough happened one night while he was jamming at a place called Dan Wall's Chili House. According to Parker:

> *I kept thinking there's bound to be something else. I could hear it but I couldn't play it.... I was working over "Cherokee," and as I did, I found that by using the higher intervals of a chord as a melody line and backing them with appropriately related [chord] changes, I could play the thing I'd been hearing. I came alive.*[4]

Parker took part in jam sessions at Minton's Playhouse and Clark Monroe's Uptown House, two nightclubs in Harlem. Among the musicians he jammed with were trumpeter Dizzy Gillespie, pianist Thelonious Monk, and drummer Kenny Clarke. According to Gillespie, "When Charlie Parker came to New York, he had just what we needed. He had the line and he had the rhythm. The way he got from one note to the other and the way he played the rhythm fit what we were trying to do perfectly. We heard him and knew the music had to go *his* way."[5]

According to drummer Kenny Clarke:

> *Bird was playing stuff we never heard before. He was into figures I thought I'd invented for drums. He was twice as fast as Lester Young and into harmony Lester hadn't even touched. Bird was running the same way we were, but he was way out ahead of us. I don't think he was aware of the changes he had created.*

Charlie Parker

Charlie Parker, known as "Bird," on the saxophone. He developed a unique way of playing jazz.

It was his way of playing jazz, part of his own experience.[6]

The new musical style of jazz Parker and the others played came to be known as bebop. The music was characterized by dazzling high-speed improvisations, complex melody lines, and sophisticated harmonies. The bebop musicians wanted to play music that was so difficult that other musicians could not copy it. At his best, Parker could play hundreds of notes per minute.

According to Studs Terkel, bebop "didn't happen overnight. Neither did it come out of a void. Bebop was a progression from the jazz forms that preceded it. It drew from all the musical traditions that had been part of the Black experience in America—and from its African roots."[7]

For the next few years, Parker played alto sax with various groups. In 1943 he played with pianist Earl "Fatha" Hines, and the following year with singer Billy Eckstine's band. Dizzy Gillespie was in both of those bands. Parker and Gillespie left Eckstine's band and went to California, where they played for a while at a Hollywood club.

When Gillespie went back to New York, Parker formed his own small group, which featured Miles Davis on trumpet. Davis was one of the younger jazz musicians who admired Parker and sought to emulate his style. Meanwhile, the Los Angeles music critics and the public did not react favorably to Parker's music. Feeling pressured, Parker sought solace in alcohol and drugs. One day he set fire to his hotel room bed. Suffering a nervous breakdown, not his first and certainly not his last, Parker was committed to Camarillo State Hospital.

Six months later, Parker was released from the hospital and traveled back to New York. He began performing

62

Birdland, the jazz club named for Charlie "Bird" Parker

and recording with some of the greatest jazz musicians of the day, including Miles Davis and Max Roach. For the next nine years, Parker was the most influential player in jazz. In spite of a difficult personal life that included two more failed marriages, two suicide attempts, the death of his young daughter, numerous mental and emotional breakdowns, and addiction to drugs and dependence on alcohol, Parker proved to the world that he was indeed a musical genius.

During the last nine years of his life, Parker played in the best jazz clubs in the United States and made three European tours. Among his greatest recordings are the tunes "KoKo," "Chasin' the Bird," "Ornithology," "Yardbird Suite," and "Scrapple From the Apple." A 1949 album, *Charlie Parker With Strings*, featuring the tune "April in Paris," was particularly successful. That year, a jazz club in New York at the corner of Fifty-Third Street and Broadway was named after Parker—Birdland.

Charlie Parker's last public performance was on March 5, 1955, at Birdland. Seven days later, he died of cirrhosis of the liver and a heart attack. He was only thirty-four years old. In a relatively few short years, Parker had done so much to change the direction of jazz. Many have attempted to explain just how he was able to do it. But no explanation was fully adequate. Perhaps Bird's own explanation is the most useful: "It's just music. It's playing clean and looking for the pretty notes."[8]

Charlie Parker Timeline

August 29, 1920—Charles Christopher Parker, Jr., is born in Kansas City, Kansas.

1936—Parker marries Rebecca Ruffin.

1939—Parker goes to New York and gets a job with pianist Jay McShann's band. Stays with band until 1942.

1943—Parker plays with pianist Earl "Fatha" Hines.

1944—Parker works with singer Billy Eckstine's band. Dizzy Gillespie is in the band.

1945—Parker and Gillespie leave Eckstine's band and go to California, where they play at a Hollywood club. Club gig is a flop. Gillespie goes back to New York. Parker is committed to Camarillo State Hospital for six months.

1949—Birdland, a jazz club named after Charlie "Bird" Parker, opens in New York.

1947–1955—Parker plays in best jazz clubs in United States and makes three European tours.

March 5, 1955—Parker makes his last public performance, at Birdland in New York.

March 12, 1955—Charlie Parker dies in New York.

1995—U.S. Postal Service issues a stamp honoring Charlie Parker.

Chapter 6

Miles Davis

Miles Davis's parents knew their son loved music. His mother encouraged him to play the violin. On his thirteenth birthday, his father bought him a new trumpet. His parents wanted him to play classical music, not jazz. But young Miles Davis was drawn to the music of Louis Armstrong and Duke Ellington, not classical music. And he would grow up to become one of the greatest and most influential jazz trumpet players of all time.

Miles Dewey Davis III was born on May 26, 1926, in Alton, Illinois, to Miles Davis II and Cleota Mae (Henry) Davis. He was raised in East St. Louis, Illinois, across the Mississippi River from St. Louis, Missouri. Miles and his sister, Dorothy, and brother, Vernon, grew up in a spacious home staffed with maids, cooks, and yardmen. Their father was a dentist, and the family lived in an integrated suburban neighborhood. Dr. Davis raised horses on his large gentleman's farm in Arkansas. There the Davis children spent happy summers.

Miles Davis,
photographed
around 1970

Miles took his first trumpet lessons from Elwood Buchanan, a local trumpet teacher. Buchanan taught Miles to develop a pure, clear tone without using vibrato. Vibrato is a quivering or pulsating effect created by slight and rapid variations in pitch. At the time, most trumpet players such as Louis Armstrong and Roy Eldridge were using vibrato, and this was the popular trumpet sound of the day. Although Miles greatly admired the music of the leading jazz trumpet players, he always stuck to his own vibrato-free sound. Throughout his career, the various unique styles of jazz he would create would feature his signature clear sound.

Miles worked hard practicing his trumpet throughout his years in high school. He got a job with a local dance band, Eddie Randle's Blue Devils. One day, Miles got to hear Billy Eckstine's band, featuring Dizzy Gillespie on trumpet and Charlie "Bird" Parker on alto sax. Eckstine and his group, touring the country, were playing a gig in East St. Louis. Miles was blown away by Dizzy and Bird, whose playing suggested a whole new world of musical possibilities.

As soon as Miles graduated from high school, he decided to go to New York, where the most exciting developments in jazz were occurring. Miles applied to the Juilliard School of Music in Manhattan and was accepted. In September 1944, his new life in New York began. Juilliard was an excellent music school, and many talented musicians from all over studied there. But at the time, Juilliard's main focus was training and producing world-class classical musicians. And Miles was mainly interested in jazz. So while he attended classes during the day, at night Miles hung out at jazz clubs. He dropped out of school after one semester.

According to writer Bob Belden, during this time Miles became friends with Charlie Parker:

> *Soon they were rooming together. Parker took Davis around with him everywhere. By the winter of 1945, Davis was a member of Parker's quintet. Playing night after night with Parker was a significant experience for Davis, and the lessons in the jazz life were to stay with him for the rest of his life.* [1]

At first, Davis was thrilled but also scared to be playing a bebop style of jazz with musicians of the caliber of Bird and Dizzy. According to Davis:

> *I was so nervous on that first real gig with Bird that I used to ask if I could quit every night. I had sat in with him, but this was my first real paying gig with him. I would ask, "What do you need me for?" ... but he would always encourage me to stay by saying that he needed me and that he loved the way I played. I hung in there and learned. I knew everything Dizzy was playing. I think that's why Bird hired me—also because he wanted a different kind of trumpet sound. Some things Dizzy played I could play, and other things he played, I couldn't. So, I just didn't play those licks that I knew I couldn't play, because I realized early on that I had to have my own voice—whatever that voice was—on the instrument.* [2]

In 1948, after three years of touring and recording with Parker, Davis formed his own band. Among the musicians in the band were Gerry Mulligan on baritone sax, Lee Konitz on alto sax, J. J. Johnson and Kai Winding on trombones, Max Roach on drums, and pianist-arranger-composer Gil Evans. The band had a different "cool" sound, subdued and delicate, rather than loud or brassy. Davis was responsible for an important element of what would be called "cool jazz"—his use of silence. Davis knew that space—the absence of playing—was as important as

sound. Each carefully selected note would have all the more impact if room was left for it to resonate. So during his solos—spare lines of improvised melody consisting of relatively few notes—Davis would allow several beats to pass without playing. The group's three recording sessions in 1949–1950 were released as *Birth of the Cool.* Many musicians were influenced by Davis's cool style, which was especially popular on the West Coast.

Meanwhile, back in New York, Davis was moving on to another style of jazz, which became known as hard bop. This rhythm-and-blues-based jazz was not quite as frantic as bebop but was more passionate than cool jazz. According to writer Grover Sales, "It is ironic that Miles Davis, a founding father of 'cool,' was among the first to drive a nail into its coffin with a 1954 recording of "Walkin'."[3] The hard-driving rhythm of "Walkin'," a twelve-bar blues, was a huge contrast to the mellow mood of West Coast jazz.

During the early 1950s, Davis struggled with a narcotics addiction. He broke the habit and performed at the Newport Jazz Festival in 1955, where he was a big hit. Davis formed a quintet, which included John Coltrane on tenor sax, Red Garland on piano, Philly Joe Jones on drums, and Paul Chambers on bass. The quintet made several recordings. In 1958, Davis added Julian "Cannonball" Adderley to the group, and they recorded the album *Milestones.*

The following year the group recorded *Kind of Blue,* which featured Bill Evans on piano. The album became one of the best-selling jazz albums of all time. Four million copies had been sold by 2009, and jazz fans continued to buy about five thousand copies a week.[4] It was the first album to popularize what would become known as "modal jazz." Instead of having solos based on

Miles Davis

Miles Davis, about 1960. As a young musician, he was nervous
playing with such greats as Charlie Parker and Dizzy Gillespie.

the chord changes of a tune, modal jazz is characterized by improvisation based on modes, various kinds of scales dating to ancient times.

In 1965, Davis recorded the album *E.S.P.* with his new band consisting of Herbie Hancock on piano, Tony Williams on drums, Wayne Shorter on tenor sax, and Ron Carter on bass. Davis continued to use the modal approach to improvisation. Many more recordings would follow.

By the late 1960s, Davis realized that rock music was displacing jazz. Artists such as Jimi Hendrix and Sly Stone had millions of fans and were drawing huge crowds. According to writer John Fordham, "Davis tried to recapture the young black audience which was drifting away from jazz."[5] Davis formed a band in which the musicians would use electric instruments. The new music they played would be a fusion of jazz and rock, with a funky soul feel. Herbie Hancock was one of several pianists to play electric piano in Davis's band. Others included Keith Jarrett, Chick Corea, and Joe Zawinul. Drummer Jack DeJohnette replaced Tony Williams, and guitarist John McLaughlin also recorded with the group. Davis's albums *In a Silent Way* and *Bitches Brew* were two of the most successful jazz-rock fusion albums.

In the late 1970s, Davis took a break from music. Various health problems and a drug addiction caught up with him. He did not touch his trumpet from 1975 to 1979. During this time, Davis met the actress Cicely Tyson. She is credited with helping him through this difficult period. The two were married in 1981. That year Davis performed at the Newport Jazz Festival to critical acclaim. Davis and Tyson divorced in 1988.

Miles Davis playing at the Beacon Theatre in New York in 1986. After taking time off due to health problems, he returned to performing in 1991.

For the next ten years, Davis continued to record fusion albums that made increased use of electronic instruments and sounds and used musical material from current pop hits. In July 1991, Davis performed with Quincy Jones at the Montreux Jazz Festival. There, for the first time in decades, he performed his hits from the 1940s and 1950s. On September 28, 1991, Miles Davis died from a stroke, pneumonia, and respiratory failure in Santa Monica, California.

Among those who recognize Davis's amazing accomplishments as an improviser, composer, and bandleader is writer Bob Belden. He wrote:

> *Davis's music connects the swing era to the hip-hop and rap world, and his innovations and groundbreaking actions have inspired and influenced countless composers, arrangers, instrumentalists, and critics. The legacy of Miles Davis will continue to be held in high regard by musicians and fans all over the world.*[6]

Miles Davis Timeline

May 26, 1926—Miles Dewey Davis III is born in Alton, Illinois.

1944—Davis enters Juilliard School of Music in New York City.

1945–1948—Davis plays with Charlie Parker's band.

1948—Davis forms his own band with Lee Konitz on alto sax, J. J. Johnson and Kai Winding on trombones, Max Roach on drums, and pianist-arranger-composer Gil Evans.

1949–1950—Davis's group's three recordings sessions are released as *Birth of the Cool*.

1955—Davis is a big hit at Newport Jazz Festival. He forms a quintet with John Coltrane on tenor sax, Red Garland on piano, Philly Joe Jones on drums, and Paul Chambers on bass.

1958—Davis adds Julian "Cannonball" Adderley to his group; they record *Milestones*.

1959—Davis records *Kind of Blue*, featuring Bill Evans on piano.

1965—Davis records the album *E.S.P.* with a new band consisting of Herbie Hancock on piano, Tony Williams on drums, Wayne Shorter on tenor sax, and Ron Carter on bass. Music features modal approach to improvising.

Late 1960s—Davis forms band in which musicians use electric instruments. He records *In a Silent Way* and *Bitches Brew*, two of the most successful jazz-rock fusion albums.

1981—Davis marries actress Cicely Tyson.

1988—Davis and Tyson are divorced.

1990—Davis receives a Grammy Lifetime Achievement Award.

1991—Davis performs with Quincy Jones at Montreux Jazz Festival.

September 28, 1991—Miles Davis dies.

2006—Davis is inducted into the Rock and Roll Hall of Fame.

2009—Fiftieth anniversary commemoration of Davis's *Kind of Blue* is held at Lincoln Center in New York City.

John Coltrane

John Coltrane's early life was filled with music and religion. Both of his parents were the children of Methodist ministers. His grandfather, the Reverend William Blair, held a very strong influence over the family. According to Coltrane:

> In my early years, we went to church every Sunday and stuff like that. We were under the influence of my grandfather, he was the dominant cat in the family. He was most well-versed, active politically ... pretty militant.... I grew up in that [and] I guess I just accepted it.[1]

Both of his parents were also amateur musicians. John's father's musical habits in particular had a tremendous influence on him. According to John's cousin Mary Lyerly:

> His father played violin and guitar in his room.... I don't think I ever saw him outside the room, but he was always playing—as soon as he came home, before dinner he would relax. The same thing that John did in later years practicing ... the very same thing. John's mother played piano, but I think he got a lot of that music from his father.[2]

John Coltrane in 1957

Considering his family influences, it comes as no surprise that throughout his life, John Coltrane would see a powerful connection between music and religion. Indeed, Coltrane would one day come to see his life as a spiritual journey in which he would create music powerful enough to improve the lives of his listeners. And Coltrane did in fact become one of the most influential jazz musicians of all time.

John William Coltrane was born in Hamlet, North Carolina, on September 23, 1926, to Alice and John Coltrane. He grew up in nearby High Point. In 1939, John joined his school's band, where he learned to play the clarinet. But once he heard a recording of saxophonist Lester Young, he switched to alto sax. And he devoted himself to practicing and mastering the instrument. According to a classmate at the time, "He kept that saxophone with him. You could hear him all the time, from any other part of the [school] building, back in the music room practicing by himself."[3]

Within a few months of John's starting on the saxophone, tragedy struck the Coltrane family. John's father died of stomach cancer. Shortly after that, the Reverend Blair and his wife passed away. And then, John's uncle, his cousin Mary's father, also died. The grief was almost too much for John to bear. The one thing that helped John through this difficult time was his saxophone. According to his biographer Lewis Porter, "In a sense, music became his father substitute."[4]

During John's senior year in high school, his mother, Aunt Bettie, and cousin Mary moved to Philadelphia to find work. In June 1943, after graduating, John joined his family in Philadelphia, where he got a job at a Campbell's Soup factory. He began taking sax lessons and classes in music theory. He modeled his sound on that of

Johnny Hodges, the alto saxophonist in Duke Ellington's orchestra.

John became friends with tenor saxophonist Benny Golson, and the two practiced together. On June 5, 1945, the two saw Charlie Parker perform with Dizzy Gillespie. Coltrane was inspired by the new bebop jazz and by Parker, who became his idol. According to Coltrane, "A big break with the dancing tradition of jazz came in the forties with Diz and Bird. You got broken rhythms, complicated harmonic devices. There [was] so much beauty … in this music."[5]

Coltrane joined the Naval Reserve in 1945 and was stationed in Honolulu. When he got out the following year, he continued his music studies back in Philadelphia at Granoff Studios. Coltrane was determined to become a professional musician and to learn as much as he could. According to his teacher Dennis Sandole, Coltrane was a "perfect student … in the conservatory he'd walk around with the horn all day long, playing."[6]

During the late 1940s, Coltrane continued to study jazz while playing rhythm-and-blues gigs in local clubs. In September 1949 he joined Dizzy Gillespie's big band, where he would work for the next eighteen months. Unfortunately around this time, like many other jazz musicians, Coltrane began using heroin.

In 1955, Coltrane married Juanita Naima Grubb, known as Naima. Also that year, Coltrane, now called "Trane" by musicians who knew him, joined Miles Davis's band. His solo on the group's recording of "'Round Midnight" drew widespread praise from critics. According to Davis:

John Coltrane playing the soprano sax at the Newport Jazz Festival in 1966—a sound that Miles Davis compared to a wailing human voice.

Trane was the loudest, fastest saxophonist I've ever heard. He could play real fast and real loud at the same time and that's very difficult to do.... But Trane could do it and he was phenomenal. It was like he was possessed when he put that horn in his mouth. He was so passionate—fierce—and yet so quiet and gentle when he wasn't playing. A sweet guy.[7]

In 1957, Coltrane's drug use began causing problems. Davis fired Coltrane because of his unreliability. With the help of his wife and his mother, Coltrane kicked his addiction to heroin. According to Coltrane, "During the year 1957, I experienced, by the grace of God, a spiritual awakening which was to lead me to a richer, fuller, more productive life."[8]

Coltrane worked with Thelonious Monk and then played again with Davis. At this time, according to writer Lewis Porter, "It was a very different Coltrane, one who played with uninhibited emotion, impressive authority, and dazzling virtuosity."[9] "Sheets of sound" is how one critic described Coltrane's style.

In 1959, Coltrane played on Davis's album *Kind of Blue*. He also recorded his own album *Giant Steps*. Coltrane then moved away from bebop and developed a modal style of improvising. Around this time, Coltrane began playing the soprano saxophone. According to Davis, "When he played the soprano, after a while it sounded almost like a human voice, wailing."[10]

In the 1960s, Coltrane recorded many albums. Accompanying Coltrane on some of his most successful albums were McCoy Tyner on piano, Jimmy Garrison on bass, and Elvin Jones on drums. One of these albums, *A Love Supreme*, recorded in December 1964, is considered by many critics to be one of the greatest jazz recordings of all time.

John Coltrane plays in Paris in 1963

In 1966, Coltrane and his wife Naima were divorced. Later that year, he married Alice McCleod. On Coltrane's last recordings, Alice plays piano. Alice Coltrane would go on to have her own career as a jazz pianist and harpist.

Coltrane continued to practice in every spare moment, never quite satisfied with his level of musicianship. His interest in modal improvisation led him to the music of many other parts of the world, including the Middle East, Africa, and India. He was especially impressed with the music of Ravi Shankar; he named his second son Ravi.

Coltrane, in his later years, also experimented with an approach to jazz that came to be called "free jazz." Free jazz songs had a loose or nonexistent structure. The music tended to sound chaotic, and many jazz lovers did not respond favorably to it. To some, free jazz sounded like noise. Horn players would purposely overblow to produce moans, shrieks, and cries. Coltrane's last recordings, however, have a mystical, meditative quality.

On July 17, 1967, John Coltrane died in New York of liver cancer. He lived his life in service to music and humanity. According to Coltrane,

> When you begin to see the possibilities of music, you desire to do something really good for people, to help humanity free itself from its hangups. I think music can make the world better and, if I'm qualified, I want to do it. I'd like to point out to people the divine in a musical language that transcends words. I want to speak to their souls.[11]

John Coltrane Timeline

September 23, 1926—John William Coltrane is born in Hamlet, North Carolina.

1939—Coltrane joins his school band in High Point, Carolina, where he learns to play clarinet.

1943—Coltrane joins family in Philadelphia after graduating. He begins taking sax lessons and classes in music theory.

1945—Coltrane sees Charlie Parker perform with Dizzy Gillespie and is inspired by new bebop jazz; joins Naval Reserve and is stationed in Honolulu.

1946—Coltrane continues music studies in Philadelphia at Granoff Studios.

September 1949—Coltrane joins Gillespie's big band.

1955—Coltrane marries Juanita Naima Grubb and joins Miles Davis's band.

1959—Coltrane plays on Davis's album *Kind of Blue*. He also records his own album *Giant Steps*.

1960s—Coltrane records many albums with McCoy Tyner on piano, Jimmy Garrison on bass, and Elvin Jones on drums. Coltrane plays a style known as free jazz.

1964—Coltrane records *A Love Supreme*, considered by many to be one of the greatest jazz recordings of all time.

July 17, 1967—John Coltrane dies in New York.

1995—U.S. Postal Service issues a stamp honoring Coltrane.

2007—Coltrane's home in Dix Hill, New York, is designated a National Historical Landmark.

2008—Fiftieth anniversary tribute to Coltrane's music is held at Lincoln Center, New York City.

Chapter 8

Herbie Hancock

" I started at seven years old, and when I was eleven, I performed at a young people's concert with the Chicago Symphony. I played the first movement of a Mozart concerto. In fact, I studied classical piano all the way through college, until I was twenty."[1]

Herbie Hancock, a child prodigy at the piano, seemed headed for a career as a classical concert pianist. But his love for jazz pulled him in a different direction. As a result, Hancock embarked on a long, successful career as a jazz pianist and composer that has spanned five decades. He has moved from one musical style to another, including hard bop, post-bop, modal music, fusion, funk, and electronic jazz-funk. In the process, he has brought enjoyment to millions of fans around the world.

Herbert Jeffrey Hancock was born on April 12, 1940, in Chicago, Illinois. His first piano teacher was a Mrs. Whalen, who gave lessons at the Ebeneezer Baptist Church in Chicago. According to Hancock, "She taught me how to read, but I had no sound, no feeling for music. Then when I was ten, I went to a Mrs. Jordan…. She

Herbie Hancock,
photographed
in 2009

realized that everything I played sounded the same. She showed me how to play nuances on the keyboard and talked in more philosophical terms, trying to get me to understand what music was all about. That's when I started getting a touch."[2]

Herbie taught himself harmony and ear training by listening to records of the great pianists Oscar Peterson and George Shearing. He listened carefully to their solos, transcribed them, and learned how to play them on the piano. He also studied the harmonies of the vocal group the Hi-Lo's, whom he admired. At Grinnell College in Iowa, Herbie took a double major in electrical engineering and music. He breezed through the music theory courses because he had already learned so much on his own.

After leaving Grinnell in 1960, Hancock worked in the post office in Chicago, while at the same time playing with saxophonist Coleman Hawkins. In December of that year, he became a member of trumpet player Donald Byrd's band. Hancock moved to New York, where he and Byrd were roommates and became friends.

In 1963, Hancock recorded his debut album, *Takin' Off*, which featured "Watermelon Man," a big hit on jazz and rhythm-and-blues radio. Apparently, the album brought Hancock to the attention of Miles Davis. In May 1963, Hancock heard rumors that Davis might be interested in him. According to Hancock, Donald Byrd said, "Look, if Miles calls you and asks if you're working with anybody, tell him no, and take the gig. More power to you. I don't want to stand in the way of your moving forward."[3] Hancock did in fact get the call, and he left Donald Byrd's band to play with Davis.

During his five years with Davis, Hancock and the group recorded successful albums such as *E.S.P.*, *Nefertiti*, and *Sorcerer*. In addition to Hancock, the group featured

89

Davis on trumpet, Wayne Shorter on tenor saxophone, Ron Carter on bass, and Tony Williams on drums. While playing with this group, Hancock began playing the Fender Rhodes electric piano. He also made other records during this time, including his jazz hit "Maiden Voyage."

On August 31, 1968, Hancock got married. He and his wife, Gudrun Meixner, went to Brazil for their honeymoon. They were due back in two weeks, in time for Hancock's next gig with Miles. Unfortunately, Hancock got food poisoning while in Brazil. The doctors would not let him leave on time because he was on medication. So when he eventually got back to New York, he found that Davis had replaced him with pianist Chick Corea. Hancock was not pleased with this development, even though he had been planning to eventually leave Davis to pursue other projects. However, even after leaving Davis's band, Hancock appeared on that group's albums *In a Silent Way* and *Bitches Brew*, recordings that marked the birth of jazz-rock fusion.

Hancock was increasingly drawn to funk, music he associated with artists such as James Brown, Sly Stone, and certain songs of Stevie Wonder. Hancock formed a group called the Headhunters, which used synthesizers. In 1973, Hancock's album *Head Hunters* became the first jazz album to go platinum—that is, to sell one million copies. It featured the hit single "Chameleon," influenced by Sly Stone.

90

By the mid-1970s, Hancock had achieved incredible success. He was playing for stadium-sized crowds all over the world, and he had at least four albums in the pop charts at once. Hancock's music from the 1970s would influence hip-hop and dance music artists that followed almost twenty years later. While immersed in the world of electronic jazz funk, Hancock continued to perform

Herbie Hancock at the piano at a jazz festival in London in 1979. His music from the 1970s would influence hip-hop and dance music decades later.

acoustic jazz with musicians such as trumpeter Freddie Hubbard and pianists Chick Corea and Oscar Peterson.

Since the 1970s, Hancock has continued to explore various styles of music, with an accent on funky rhythms. He has composed film scores and music for TV. In 1980, he introduced the trumpeter Wynton Marsalis to the world. He produced Marsalis's debut album and toured with him. In 1986 Hancock won an Oscar for scoring the film *'Round Midnight*, in which he also appeared as an actor. *'Round Midnight* tells the story of fictional African-American jazzman Dale Turner and his struggle with alcohol abuse in Paris during the 1950s. In 1998, Hancock recorded *Gershwin's World*. Appearing with him were Stevie Wonder, Joni Mitchell, Kathleen Battle, Wayne Shorter, and Chick Corea, among others. *Gershwin's World* won three Grammys in 1999.

One common aspect of Hancock's recording projects is that, especially in recent years, each new album is stylistically different from the previous one. Hancock believes in never being afraid to try new things, even if this means not pleasing the critics. According to Hancock:

> *Actually, for me, criticism is an indication that I'm doing something right. If I'm not being challenged then maybe I'm working in an area where I'm too comfortable. People aren't always able to rise to the occasion themselves and end up working inside their comfort zone. That can also be true for critics.*[4]

In 2005, Hancock recorded the album *Possibilities*, a collaboration with many artists including Sting, Annie Lennox, John Mayer, Christina Aguilera, Paul Simon, Carlos Santana, Joss Stone, and Damien Rice. In 2007 he recorded *River: The Joni Letters*, which featured jazz treatments of the music of Joni Mitchell. In addition to Mitchell, it includes artists such as Norah Jones and

Herbie Hancock with the Grammy awards he won in 2008. He has won twelve Grammys over the years for his jazz recordings.

Tina Turner. Hancock says that on this album, for the first time in his career, he focused on the meaning of the lyrics. Hancock has won twelve Grammy awards for his jazz performances. On January 18, 2009, he had the honor of performing at the opening celebration for the presidential inauguration of Barack Obama at the Lincoln Memorial in Washington, D.C.

Herbie Hancock is open to all types of music and does not believe in putting albums in categories. His goal is to create music that many people will want to listen to. He wants to make his listeners happy. According to Hancock:

> *I don't have any message to give anyone. I want to inspire people, just to do better at what they're doing. If I can make people feel good tonight so that tomorrow they'll go to work with smiles on their faces, then my music is valuable. It's people who determine value.*[5]

Herbie Hancock Timeline

April 12, 1940—Herbert Jeffrey Hancock is born in Chicago, Illinois.

1947—Hancock begins taking piano lessons.

1951—Hancock performs at a young people's concert with the Chicago Symphony.

1960—Hancock leaves Grinnell College and moves back to Chicago. He then joins trumpet player Donald Byrd's band and moves to New York.

1963—Hancock records debut album, *Takin' Off*, featuring "Watermelon Man." Later that year he joins Miles Davis's band.

1968—Hancock marries Gudrun Meixner. Davis replaces Hancock with Chick Corea.

1970s—Hancock, increasingly drawn to electronic jazz and funk, uses synthesizers and other electronics.

1973—Hancock's album *Headhunters* is first jazz album to go platinum. It features hit single "Chameleon."

1980—Hancock produces Wynton Marsalis's debut album and tours with him.

1986—Hancock wins an Oscar for scoring the film *'Round Midnight*.

1998—Hancock records *Gershwin's World*, which wins three Grammys in 1999.

2005—Hancock records *Possibilities* in collaboration with many famous artists.

2007—Hancock records *River: The Joni Letters*, featuring jazz treatments of the music of Joni Mitchell.

2009—Hancock performs at the concert opening the inaugural activities for President Barack Obama.

Discography: Two Notable Recordings by Each Artist

Louis Armstrong

The Definitive Collection

2006 (original recording remastered)
Hip-O Records B000CQQHFO
23 of Armstrong's greatest hits

The Hot Fives and Sevens

(4-disc set) 1999
JSP Records B00001ZWLP
89 examples of Armstrong's Dixieland jazz from the 1920s

Duke Ellington

The Essential Duke Ellington

(2-disc set) 2005 (original recording remastered)
Sony B0009RQSC8
37 of Ellington's greatest songs

Black, Brown and Beige

1999 (original recording remastered)
Sony B000001MYC
Ellington's long-form concert piece, featuring Mahalia
   Jackson on vocal parts

Ella Fitzgerald

Pure Ella: The Very Best of Ella Fitzgerald

1994
Verve B00000690N
18 of Fitzgerald's greatest hits

Ella Fitzgerald: The Best of the Song Books

1993
Verve B0000046R2

Dizzy Gillespie

Night in Tunisia: The Very Best of Dizzy Gillespie

2006 (original recording remastered)
RCA B000G7PNFY
14 of Gillespie's greatest hits

Groovin' High

1994
Legacy International B000005OAS

Charlie Parker

The Best of Charlie Parker: 20th Century Masters—The Millennium Collection

2004 (original recording remastered)
Verve B0002M5T5M
11 of Parker's finest recordings

Charlie Parker with Strings: The Master Takes

1995
Polygram Records B0000046WK
24 songs with Parker accompanied by a small string
   orchestra

Discography: Two Notable Recordings by Each Artist

Miles Davis

Kind of Blue

1959 (original recording reissued, remastered)
Sony B000002ADT
One of the best-selling jazz albums of all time

Birth of the Cool

1956 (original recording reissued, remastered)
Blue Note Records B00005614M

John Coltrane

A Love Supreme

1964 (original recording reissued, remastered)
Impulse Records B0000A118M
Considered one of the greatest jazz recordings ever

My Favorite Things

1961 (original recording reissued)
Atlantic / WEA B000002153

Herbie Hancock

The Essential Herbie Hancock

(2-disc set) 2006 (original recording remastered)
Sony B000E6EJ7U
20-tune collection shows how Hancock successfully
    crossed the boundaries of jazz and pop for four decades

River: The Joni Letters

2007
Verve B000UVLK1M
Hancock's reimagining of Joni Mitchell's music

Chapter Notes

Introduction

1. Bill Kirchner, ed., *Oxford Companion to Jazz* (New York: Oxford University Press, 2000), p. 3.
2. James Haskins, *Black Music in America: A History Through Its People* (New York: Thomas Y. Crowell, 1987), p. 37.
3. Ibid., p. 44.
4. Grover Sales, *Jazz: America's Classical Music* (Englewood Cliffs, N.J.: Prentice Hall, 1984), p. 13.
5. Ted Gioia, *The History of Jazz* (New York: Oxford University Press, 1997), p. 395.

Chapter 1
Louis Armstrong

1. Geoffrey C. Ward and Ken Burns, *Jazz: A History of America's Music* (New York: Alfred A. Knopf, 2000), pp. 41–42.
2. Ibid., p. 40.
3. Robert Gottlieb, ed., *Reading Jazz: A Gathering of Autobiography, Reportage, and Criticism from 1919 to Now* (New York: Pantheon Books, 1996), p. 23.
4. Ward and Burns, p. 115.
5. Ibid., p. 117.

Chapter 2
Duke Ellington

1. David Bradbury, *Duke Ellington* (London: Haus Publishing, 2005), p. 4.
2. Ted Gioia, *The History of Jazz* (New York: Oxford University Press, 1997), p. 118.
3. Bradbury, p. 17.
4. Gioia, p. 122.

5. Geoffrey C. Ward and Ken Burns, *Jazz: A History of America's Music* (New York: Alfred A. Knopf, 2000), p. 118.

Chapter 3
Ella Fitzgerald

1. Robert Gottlieb, ed., *Reading Jazz: A Gathering of Autobiography, Reportage, and Criticism from 1919 to Now* (New York: Pantheon Books, 1996), pp. 980–981.
2. Tanya Lee Stone, *Ella Fitzgerald* (New York: Viking, 2008), p. 25.
3. Stuart Nicholson, *Ella Fitzgerald: A Biography of the First Lady of Jazz* (New York: Da Capo Press, 1995), p. 5.
4. Ibid., p. 13.
5. Ibid., p. 12.
6. Stone, p. 19.
7. Bill Kirchner, ed., *Oxford Companion to Jazz* (New York: Oxford University Press, 2000), p. 241.

Chapter 4
Dizzy Gillespie

1. Ted Gioia, *The History of Jazz* (New York: Oxford University Press, 1997), p. 209.
2. Robert Gottlieb, ed., *Reading Jazz: A Gathering of Autobiography, Reportage, and Criticism from 1919 to Now* (New York: Pantheon Books, 1996), p. 600.
3. Studs Terkel, *Giants of Jazz* (New York: Thomas Crowell Company, 1975), p. 155.
4. Billy Taylor, *Jazz Piano: A Jazz History* (Dubuque, Iowa: Wm. C. Brown Company Publishers, 1982), p. 143.

5. John Fordham, *Jazz* (New York: Dorling Kindersley, 1993), p. 113.
6. Ibid.
7. Terkel, p. 161.

Chapter 5
Charlie Parker

1. Bill Kirchner, ed., *Oxford Companion to Jazz* (New York: Oxford University Press, 2000), p. 319.
2. Ibid., p. 320.
3. Studs Terkel, *Giants of Jazz* (New York: Thomas Crowell Company, 1975), p. 164.
4. John Fordham, *Jazz* (New York: Dorling Kindersley, 1993), pp. 110–111.
5. Robert Gottlieb, ed., *Reading Jazz: A Gathering of Autobiography, Reportage, and Criticism from 1919 to Now* (New York: Pantheon Books, 1996), p. 1031.
6. Terkel, p. 168.
7. Ibid., p. 167.
8. Kirchner, p. 331.

Chapter 6
Miles Davis

1. Bill Kirchner, ed., *Oxford Companion to Jazz* (New York: Oxford University Press, 2000), p. 391.
2. Robert Gottlieb, ed., *Reading Jazz: A Gathering of Autobiography, Reportage, and Criticism from 1919 to Now* (New York: Pantheon Books, 1996), pp. 580–581.
3. Grover Sales, *Jazz: America's Classical Music* (Englewood Cliffs, N.J.: Prentice Hall, 1984), p. 171.
4. Malcolm Jones, "The Blue and the Great," *Newsweek*, January 31, 2009, p. 63.

5. John Fordham, *Jazz* (New York: Dorling Kindersley, 1993), p. 115.
6. Kirchner, p. 402.

Chapter 7
John Coltrane

1. Ashley Kahn, *A Love Supreme: The Story of John Coltrane's Signature Album* (New York: Viking, 2002), p. 7.
2. Ibid., p. 6.
3. Ibid., p. 8.
4. Ibid.
5. Ibid., p. 10.
6. Ibid.
7. Robert Gottlieb, ed., *Reading Jazz: A Gathering of Autobiography, Reportage, and Criticism from 1919 to Now* (New York: Pantheon Books, 1996), p. 246.
8. Bill Kirchner, ed., *Oxford Companion to Jazz* (New York: Oxford University Press, 2000), p. 436.
9. Ibid., p. 437.
10. Gottlieb, p. 247.
11. Kirchner, p. 443.

Chapter 8
Herbie Hancock

1. Len Lyons, *The Great Jazz Pianists Speaking of Their Lives and Music* (New York: Quill, 1983), p. 271.
2. Ibid., pp. 271–272.
3. Ibid., p. 272.
4. Andrew Bruse, *Herbie Hancock: Outside the Comfort Zone*, JamBase, August 14, 2007, <http://www.jambase.com/Articles/11098/Herbie-Hancock-Outside-The-Comfort-Zone/2> (May 27, 2010).
5. Lyons, p. 283.

Glossary

bar—A rhythmic unit that contains a fixed number of beats; a measure.

bebop—A style of jazz developed during the 1940s, characterized by high-speed improvising, complex melody lines, and sophisticated harmonies.

big bands—Jazz bands of one or two dozen members, especially popular during the swing era of the 1930s.

blues—A type of folk song expressing sorrow, loneliness, defiance, or humor that originated among African Americans in the Deep South at the end of the nineteenth century.

burlesque—A type of humorous show featuring musical acts and comic skits.

cool jazz—A mellow style of jazz developed during the 1950s.

free jazz—A style of jazz developed during the 1960s characterized by few or no rules; players were free to dispense with the usual elements of jazz improvisation such as melodic themes and chord patterns.

gigs—Music jobs.

honky-tonks—Cheap nightclubs or dance halls.

Glossary

jam session—An informal gathering of musicians to play music, especially improvised jazz.

jazz-rock fusion—A style of music that mixes jazz with rock, funk, and soul.

lyrics—The words to a song.

modal jazz—Jazz improvisation based on modes instead of chord changes. Modes are ancient scales used in medieval church music and Indian music.

mute—A device attached to a musical instrument to soften or muffle its tone.

octave—Eight notes of a scale.

ragtime—An African-American musical form featuring syncopated rhythms.

riffs—Short repeated rhythmic, melodic, or harmonic figures that form the basis of a musical composition.

scat singing—Vocal jazz improvisation consisting of nonsense syllables.

swing—A strong, syncopated rhythmic "groove" or feel created by playing behind or ahead of the beat; also a style of jazz popular during the 1930s and 1940s.

syncopated—Having accents or emphasis on the weak beat, or just before or after the beat.

transpose—To change a piece of music to another key.

vibrato—A quivering or pulsating effect created by slight and rapid variations in pitch.

Further Reading

Gourse, Leslie. *Sophisticated Ladies: The Great Women of Jazz*. New York: Dutton Children's Books, 2007.

Handyside, Christopher. *A History of Jazz*. Chicago: Heinemann-Raintree, 2005.

Marsalis, Wynton. *Jazz A–B–Z*. Cambridge, Mass.: Candlewick Press, 2005.

Myers, Walter Dean. *Jazz*. New York: Holiday House, 2008.

Stone, Tanya Lee. *Up Close, Ella Fitzgerald*. New York: Viking, 2008.

Teachout, Terry. *Pops: A Life of Louis Armstrong*. San Diego: Houghton Mifflin Harcourt, 2009.

Internet Addresses

Jazz for Young People Online
<http://www.jalc.org/jazzED/j4yp_curr>

PBS Kids Go! Jazz
<http://pbskids.org/jazz>

Smithsonian Jazz
<http://www.smithsonianjazz.org>

Index

Index

111

4-8-16